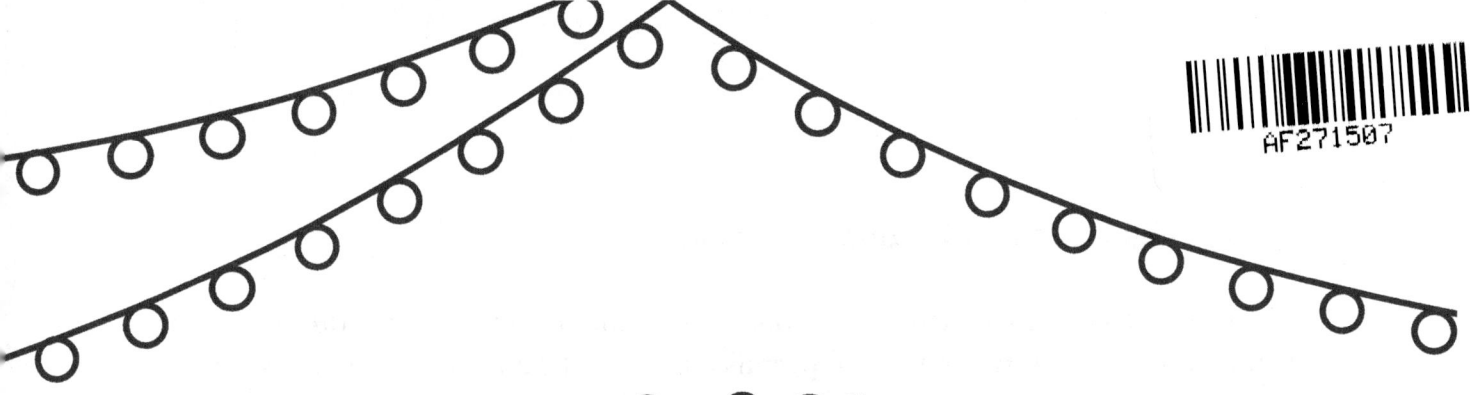

HI, I'M AUGUST

A coloring book celebrating diffrences
and inspiring inclusion for all ages.

This coloring book belongs to

. . . .

Want more inspiration and fun coloring ideas?

Follow us on instagram!

Aggibaggcoloringbooks - join our

community and celebrate inclusion with us!

WHAT DOES BEING A GOOD FRIEND MEAN TO YOU?

17

LEARN

TOGETHER WE CAN SPREAD KINDNESS AND UNDERSTANDING.

I MIGHT NOT SPEAK WITH WORDS, BUT I SPEAK WITH MY HEART

EVERYONE WITH STXBP1 ARE UNIQUE

SOMETIMES I NEED HELP AND THAT'S OKAY

BRAVE EVEN IN CHAOS

BE
KIND
ALWAYS

WOULD YOU LIKE TO SHARE?

EVERY STAR HAS ITS OWN STORY,
JUST LIKE YOU

TOGETHER WE CREATE
A WORLD WHERE
EVERYONE BELONGS

WE ARE ALL DIFFERENT AND THAT MAKES US STRONGER!

Made in the USA
Monee, IL
03 April 2025

15117423R00046